SACRED SOLOS

Compiled
Arranged and Edited
by CLAIR W. JOHNSON

for
Trombone or Baritone with Piano Accompaniment

CONTENTS

VOLUMES IN THIS SERIES

C Flute and Piano

Bb Clarinet and Piano

Bb Cornet or Trumpet (Baritone 𝄞) and Piano

Eb Alto Saxophone and Piano

Trombone or Baritone 𝄢 and Piano

Each volume varies in contents and arrangements to favor the instrument concerned.

RUBANK

HAL•LEONARD
CORPORATION
7777 W. BLUEMOUND RD. P.O. BOX 13819 MILWAUKEE, WI 53213

T0057715

If With All Your Hearts

from Elijah

FELIX MENDELSSOHN
Arr. by Clair W. Johnson

4

Prayer
from Cavalleria Rusticana

PIETRO MASCAGNI
Arr. by Clair W. Johnson

Beautiful Isle of Somewhere

J. S. FEARIS
Arr. by Clair W. Johnson

Where'er You Walk

from Semele

G. F. HANDEL
Arr. by Clair W. Johnson

Agnus Dei

GEORGES BIZET
Arr. by Clair W. Johnson

(38) Maestoso

Agnus Dei **3**

Ave Maria

FR. SCHUBERT
Arr. by Clair W. Johnson

Ave Maria 4 (Schubert)

(31) *obbligato*

Trb.

Ave Maria 4 (Schubert)

Calvary

PAUL RODNEY
Arr. by Clair W. Johnson

(24) Andante

(47) Giubiloso

(65) Andante

The Rosary

ETHELBERT NEVIN
Arr. by Clair W. Johnson

SACRED SOLOS

Compiled
Arranged and Edited
by CLAIR W. JOHNSON

for
Trombone or Baritone with Piano Accompaniment

CONTENTS

VOLUMES IN THIS SERIES

C Flute and Piano   B♭ Clarinet and Piano

B♭ Cornet or Trumpet (Baritone 𝄞) and Piano

E♭ Alto Saxophone and Piano   Trombone or Baritone 𝄢 and Piano

Each volume varies in contents and arrangements to favor the instrument concerned.

RUBANK®

HAL•LEONARD®

If With All Your Hearts

from Elijah

Trombone or Baritone

FELIX MENDELSSOHN
Arr. by Clair W. Johnson

Andante con moto

Prayer
from Cavalleria Rusticana

Trombone or Baritone

PIETRO MASCAGNI
Arr. by Clair W. Johnson

Andante sostenuto

dim. e rall.

Beautiful Isle of Somewhere

Trombone or Baritone ♉

J. S. FEARIS
Arr. by Clair W. Johnson

Where'er You Walk
from Semele

G. F. HANDEL
Arr. by Clair W. Johnson

Agnus Dei

Trombone or Baritone 𝄢

GEORGES BIZET
Arr. by Clair W. Johnson

Ave Maria

Trombone or Baritone

FR. SCHUBERT
Arr. by Clair W. Johnson

Calvary

Trombone or Baritone 𝄢

PAUL RODNEY
Arr. by Clair W. Johnson

The Rosary

ETHELBERT NEVIN
Arr. by Clair W. Johnson

Panis Angelicus

Trombone or Baritone 𝄢

CÉSAR FRANCK
Arr. by Clair W. Johnson

The Holy City

STEPHEN ADAMS
Arr. by Clair W. Johnson

Ave Maria

Trombone or Baritone 𝄢

BACH-GOUNOD
Arr. by Clair W. Johnson

Andante con moto

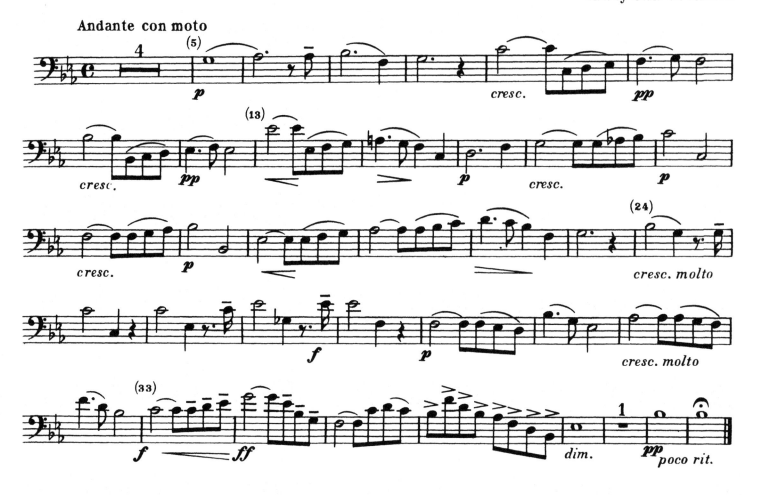

O, Divine Redeemer

CH. GOUNOD
Arr. by Clair W. Johnson

Molto moderato

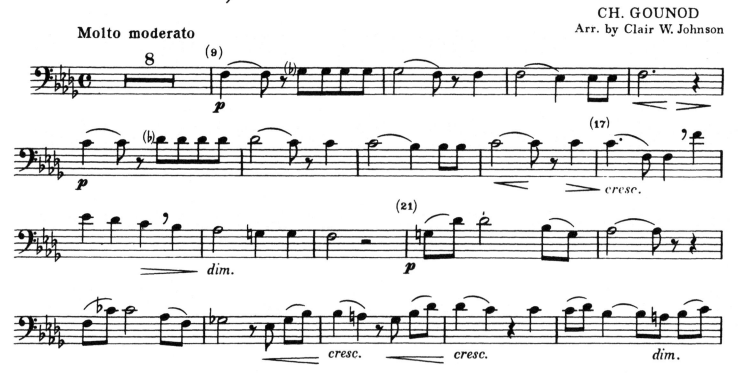

Alleluja
from Exsultate Jubilate

Trombone* or Baritone 9:

W. A. MOZART
Arr. by Clair W. Johnson

Allegro non troppo

* Trombone may play slurred passages with light legato tongue.   ** Trills may be omitted.

Panis Angelicus

CÉSAR FRANCK
Arr. by Clair W. Johnson

The Holy City

STEPHEN ADAMS
Arr. by Clair W. Johnson

34

The Holy City 5

(60)

Ave Maria

BACH - GOUNOD
Arr. by Clair W. Johnson

Ave Maria 3 (Bach-Gounod)

Ave Maria 3 (Bach-Gounod)

O, Divine Redeemer

CH. GOUNOD
Arr. by Clair W. Johnson

O, Divine Redeemer 6

Alleluja
from Exsultate Jubilate

W. A. MOZART
Arr. by Clair W. Johnson

Trombone may play slurred passages with light legato tongue.

* Trills may be omitted.

INDISPENSABLE FOLIO

By
R. M. ENDRESEN

A COLLECTION OF INTERESTING SOLOS
WITH FORMATIVE TECHNIC

Published for...

C Flute and Piano

Bb Clarinet and Piano

Bb Cornet or Trumpet and Piano

Trombone or Baritone and Piano

Eb Alto Saxophone and Piano

Bb Tenor Saxophone and Piano

Contents...

1. THE ENVOY

2. SPINNING WHEEL

3. FOX HUNT

4. MOONLIGHT SERENADE

5. WHISTLIN' PETE

6. HOLIDAY MEDLEY

7. SCHOOL MUSICIAN

8. FOREST ECHO

9. POLISH DANCE

10. VALSE CAPRICE

11. SYNCOPATOR

RUBANK®

HAL•LEONARD®
CORPORATION
7777 W. BLUEMOUND RD. P.O. BOX 13819 MILWAUKEE, WI 53213